Lo-fi Poetry Series Poet
Sounds

 Poets Cover Your Record Collection

Lo-fi Poetry Series
Poet Sounds

An Anthology Inspired by
The Beach Boys' *Pet Sounds*
Edited by
Gerry LaFemina
and
Christine Stroud

CITYLIT PRESS

Baltimore, Maryland

© 2020, CityLit Project

Library of Congress Control Number: 2019937121
ISBN: 978-1-936328-21-5
CityLit Project is a 501(c)(3) nonprofit organization
founded in 2004 to promote the literary arts
for readers and writers in the mid-Atlantic region.
Federal Tax ID Number: 20-0639118

All rights reserved. No part of this book may be
reproduced or transmitted in any form or by any means,
electronic or mechanical, including photocopy, recording,
or any information storage and retrieval system,
without prior permission from the publisher
(except by reviewers who may quote brief passages).

Printed in the United States of America | First Edition
Lo-fi Poetry Series Editors: Gerry LaFemina and Gregg Wilhelm
Cover and Book Design: Gregg Wilhelm
Cover Photograph: Maria Keifer Diehl
Gerry LaFemina, Jack DuBose, Jennifer Browne, and Alex LaFemina
read poetry to goats.

The title to M. L. Liebler's poem "The world could show nothing to me" is attributed to
Tony Asher, who co-wrote eight of the songs on the Beach Boys' *Pet Sounds* album.

c/o CityLit Project
120 W. North Avenue
Suite 201
Baltimore, MD 21201
Publisher's Contact: 410.274.5691
www.CityLitProject.org
info@citylitproject.org

"I think in terms of emotions. And feelings. So sometimes what I say may not always be clear. But creatively, there's a lot to be said for that way of thinking."

Brian Wilson

"I've got different things going on—part spiritualist, part humanitarian, part brat."

Mike Love

"I love driving; driving along the California coastline is the best drive in the world."

Al Jardine

"You know, The Beach Boys' image is kinda like a group Doris Day, you know what I mean?"

Bruce Johnston

For Jon Tribble

Set List

Sloop John B

17 / Sloop John B by John Davis
18 / Sloop John B by Dawn McDuffie

Caroline, No

21 / Where Did Her Long Hair Go? by John Davis
22 / Caroline No by Tim Kahl

Wouldn't It Be Nice

25 / Wouldn't it Be Nice by Katie Mullins
26 / Self-Portrait: Dennis by Tim Tomlinson
27 / Maybe in Monterey by Brent Royster
29 / Wouldn't It Be Nice by Jessica Server

You Still Believe in Me

35 / You Still Believe in Me by Tim Tomlinson
36 / Listening to the Beach Boys Through the Magnetic Fields
    by George Yatchisin
38 / You Still Believe in Me by Robert Balun

That's Not Me

43 / I had to prove that I could / Make it alone now, but that's by Jon Tribble
45 / That's Not Me by Denise Scannell Guida

Don't Talk (Put Your Head on My Shoulder)

49 / Don't Talk (Put Your Head on My Shoulder) by Ken Pobo
50 / Don't Talk (Put Your Head on My Shoulder) by Susana H. Case

I'm Waiting for the Day

53 / I'm Waiting for the Day by Amy Lemmon
55 / Waiting for the Day by Jon Tribble

Let's Go Away for Awhile

59 / Let's Go Away For Awhile by D. Gilson
61 / Let's Go Away for Awhile by Tim Tomlinson
62 / Let's Go Away for Awhile by Corey Oglesby
64 / Let's Go Away for Awhile by David Starkey

God Only Knows

69 / God only knows by Rishi Dastidar
70 / without you by Bonnie Emerick
71 / "The world could show nothing to me" by M. L. Liebler
72 / Only Gods Know by Sean Murphy

I Know There's an Answer

77 / I Know There's an Answer by John Davis
78 / Unlike Brian Wilson by Brendan Stephens
80 / I Know There's an Answer by Tim Tomlinson

Here Today

83 / Here Today by Susana H. Case
84 / I'm the Girl He Left Before You Found Him by Kestra Forest
86 / Here, Today by Gerry LaFemina

I Just Wasn't Made for These Times

91 / I Just Wasn't Made for These Times by Joey Nicoletti
92 / I Just Wasn't Made for These Times by Glen Armstrong

Pet Sounds

97 / Pet Sounds by John Davis
98 / Pet Sounds by Gerry LaFemina

Liner Notes

101 / Listening to Pet Sounds by Lisa Kosow
102 / When the Beach Boys Came to Wolf Trap by Jacqueline Jules
104 / Elegy for Brian Wilson's Smile by George Guida
106 / The Other Guy Speaks by Donald Illich
108 / Wilson and Love by Margaret Luongo
109 / How to Work It Out by Andrea Rogers
111 / [still] waiting for the millennium by Vincent A. Cellucci
113 / Charlie and The Beach Boys by Ned Balbo
115 / Animal Gospel by Jane Satterfield
116 / In me there's an answer, you still believe I know by Cameron McGill
118 / The Beach Boys Come in From the Beach by Lisa Kosow

Deadwax

121 / "Never Much of a Beach Boys Fan" by Gerry LaFemina
123 / "More Than Just Surfer Anthems" by Christine Stroud
127 / About the Poets
136 / About the Lo-fi Poetry Series

Sloop John B

Sloop John B

                                                    John Davis

It's a mid-July battle of the bands at the stoplight,
car windows rolled down. My yellow Ford

chunk-chunk-chunks a staccato rhythm. The seats
smell of oil. I'm blasting "Sloop John B" against "I'm a Man"

in the blue Chevy. The smirk on the driver's face
tells me I'm uncool. But I'm cool and I'm a man

listening to the Beach Boys on my 8 track.
It's a campfire song I learned roasting marshmallows.

Elbow out the window, I'm riding sloop waves.
Those high harmonies are the winds I need. I'm feeling

broke up because I'm sixteen and that's what I'm supposed
to feel, but I don't want to go home. I chicken-nod

my head, sing *do-do, do-do*, check the side view mirror
for my hint of a first beard. If I gun the engine,

it will die. In three summers I will enlist
in the Coast Guard, feel the real winds, know what

a fid is and I will want to go home. But for now
I see how the main sets and wait for the green light.

Sloop John B

Dawn McDuffie

Catamaran Cruise, Kauai

Your luck has changed, wind straight in your face
full of rain and chill. You never believed Hawaii
could be this cold, your straw sun hat overboard—
wet cotton sweater that has given up its mission.
Downstairs on the stuffy lower deck, the toilet
can't take it. You didn't taste those Mai Tais,
and you are grateful. Icy spray, salt in your eyes,
but it's fresh and smells like ocean and darkness.
The captain turns from his snug perch and calls
to eight drenched people on the upper deck,
"Come on over here." He's got his oldies tape on,
and everyone sings, "Hoist up the John B's sail.
See how the main sail sets..." You are amazed
that you can sing those beach harmonies. "Home"
has three syllables, dense with counterpoint
and longing. Everyone sings. You love the storm,
and you want to be home, not your official address
but the home you imagine, safe and dry. You
imagine cooking grits and eggs for every tired sailor.

Caroline, No

Where Did Her Long Hair Go?

John Davis

snipped into a bucket
swept up, meshed with dust
a gift for Locks of Love

or bobbed or flattened
punked-out black
with silver glitter

gone in the echo
of an empty water bottle
turned upside down

Caroline
originally Carol I Know
then Caroline No

gone to Broadway
to be a dancer
cut her hair

Carol I knew
gone like heat
that leaves the earth

Caroline No

Tim Kahl

Where did your long hair go, Caroline?
Are reports of it going missing
just another fake news story on the net?
It says those tresses of yours are now genetically
wedded to the wayward limbs of the weeping willow.
Your veins run through the petunias, my Caroline,
my plantimal that stands as strange hybrid
of the art world and medical research
like that albino bunny that glows in the dark
from the jellyfish's fluorescent protein.
Oh Caroline, no—don't say we were
fragile lovers buckling under the pressure
of external forces. Don't say we weren't
the kind of couple others would have died to be—
Oh Caroline, no. Who took that look away
and put it in the garden's Virginia creeper
so that I'm reminded of your sweet flowing mane
every time the wind messes how softly it lays?
Don't take that look away from me who has
become the eternal stomach sleeper, the one
whose handwriting always appears in miniature.
I'm caught up in my wilting ways
that I inherited from the impatiens.
I shrink from the world as it could be,
as perfect encounter between your
countenance and the perennials.
Oh Caroline, don't look at me that way.

Wouldn't It Be Nice

Wouldn't It Be Nice

Katie Mullins

When you say it now, "Wouldn't it be nice—"
I always hear it in that brilliant harmony, sunrises
and citrus-colored rainbows exploding, all
that virile optimism before "if we were older,"
like we still don't know how goddamned hard
age will be. I know the truth is closer
to the moment that lives after the needle lifts
itself off the vinyl ridges, slides slowly back home
and the static finally fades to absolute silence:
the waiting could have been the good part, baby,
that here we are now, locked in the room, lying
in bed just like Brian Wilson did.

        But I don't think I realized all those notes,
those perfect, glowing moments, shot through
with innocence, would feel so different when
the rain made our knees hurt and we couldn't eat
spicy foods before bed anymore. I didn't realize
the kind of world where we belonged was one
of our own making, cocooned in the same isolation
we had feared all those years. I don't know how
our thoughts and wishes and hopes turned into
dreaming and scheming, lying awake to pray—
but here we are. It's dark, but I'm not alone, and
I am not afraid, in our room—and there's that fade out.
Good night, baby. Sleep tight, baby.

Self-Portrait: Dennis

Tim Tomlinson

That's me in the back, at the drum kit,
flipping hair out of my eyes like Ringo.
Sometimes I don't even bother to pretend
I'm singing, or drumming. I'm chewing gum.

I'm surfing. I didn't ask to be in
the group—that was Dad's idea. Then
it was like I wasn't. The way the drums
come in on "Wouldn't It Be Nice?"

with a whomp and a flam—thanks, but that's Hal.
My skills weren't needed. No one even
noticed how I slipped away in the mornings,
bellied onto a board, paddled out.

I used to think wouldn't it be nice if
I could write a song like Brian, do something
on my own... Enter: Charles Manson. And
I know, I know. One thing though: I lived

the life they wrote about. I caught the waves.
I got the chicks. I was the one got
the fuck around. I was the happiest
man alive except for the hangovers.

It doesn't help to talk about it, but
maybe someone could have noticed, said where's
Dennis? And maybe they'd have found me before
my lungs filled up with Marina Del Rey.

Maybe in Monterey

Brent Royster

Because it's Monterey after a show at a campfire on the beach.
A girl with inevitable cigarettes and a gauzy seafoam kaftan
that's wild and everywhere, like her hair, dusty and ginger
in crazed fire light. It's a gather ye rosebuds kind of thing;
you know, world enough and time. Something to say
when young—she's young, everybody's young, the night
itself, and nobody wants to leave this party unless there's
more fit fun elsewhere. Sand-dancing slow, far from the crowd,
shadows cast on the tide. Arms around your neck, her head
drowsing, she's dreamy dreaming when she asks wouldn't it be nice,
and in the jangle of keys you're back at the flat rented up off the bay.

Moonlight on the wood floor. Sprawled deep in burnt orange shag,
head propped on a corduroy chaise, where she rests, her loose arm
draped across your chest, her face rimmed in loose hair and smoke,
the kaftan to her thigh and she's dreamy, just dreamy, dazed far off.
You ask wouldn't it be nice, fingertips spinning a stem of patchouli,
the ember and the smoke ribboning like a gymnastic tether.
She's a bird not to be nested, you know, unless. But she won't.
No Maybelline babydoll, she couldn't, can't. But wouldn't it be?
Nice? Such an honestly wholesome pose to play with countless horrible
hateful words spoken everywhere. Strangers dying, starving on beaches
that don't look like Monterey. The world burning with madness,
falling away. Monterey's scattered kids want to picture something else.

Or nothing at all. Monterey is a place to hold time, smoky, befogged,
and words, now, in darkness—a distant dream. Wouldn't it be?
You don't just want to make her. This real moment will fade, if only,
and bullets and bombs don't care about what could have been.

There's always Canada, or the countryside, or would she wait?
But who could wait so far away, the world forever collecting wounds.
You glance up and her face is on yours and suddenly the shadows
are all over the room. Something to say when young and going away.
You're both all go, but you can't, unless, if only. . . . And then
she has her fingers on your belt loops and you're practically married,
if only, except, unless. Maybe in Monterey, it doesn't matter.

Wouldn't It Be Nice

Jessica Server

*You know it seems the more we talk about it,
It only makes it worse to live without it.*

I once believed the arc of bridges, the start
and end point, spanning, spanning, spanning
the great, watery in-between. I believed in nice,
its dandelion stain inside my wrist.

Now I watch my students—14, 15, 16 years old—
wishing for nice. Breasts
and breath upon their necks, origami
whispers folded with purpose. Then folded again.

I ache for their big, blind world,
the yet-to-come firsts and faraway fears,
every mistake still glinting before them,
distant suns on slow-rolling seas.

I had it, once: the kind of love you give in
and grow up for. A kind of wood and wool
love that holds itself *close the whole night through.*
And it was nice. But also electric, soil-stained,

breathless and bruised. Tethering
and unhinging and climbing and charging
erroneous and voracious. It was beetles
and waterlogged shame. I want to tell them:

falling asleep does *make it that much better*,
leaving today on your pillow in layers
of dead skin cells. I want to tell them:
wake the fuck up. You can do better than nice.

Some days, I cry just thinking about the fire
I once lit with my body. It was nice, but also
a living, panting, animal. Sometimes, I cry
so hard that I vomit. Vomit is better

than nice, too. Bile means alive. I want
to tell them: Stop; it won't be *nice
to live together*. It will be talons and feathers
and claws. It will be rooted and burnt
raw and exquisite. You will wake

some 2 AMs and listen to the breath
beside you, to the tock of a distant kitchen
clock that you hung all by yourself,
using a stepladder, and you will weep.

One 2 AM, you may kiss a woman just to see
if it is, indeed, nice. It is. But also
baffling and hell-bent on beauty. You will learn
to forget the knots in the wood. You'll still love

*waking up in the morning when the day
is new*, but you'll wake at home in your bed
alone or in someone else's bed
alone. This is nice. This is complicated.

I want to tell them about that word, complicated:
it will be nice to say and not nice enough. Not nice
enough and not what you need and not
what you sing to yourself in the shower as you shave

your downy legs in preparation for spring's
hot arrival. You *thought* and *wished*
and *hoped* and *prayed* and it came true, but you'll
walk away from this person or that. As it turns out,

there was *a single thing* you couldn't do.
But I don't say any of it. Because until they've had
the wool and the wood, the striving and sutures,
the nights lying in wait, like fishermen, for a fresh

bite at the line, until they've squeezed themselves
into a too-tight skirt, or worn high heels only to wander
barefoot until dawn, until they've lost themselves
in the Tasman, or found themselves in the Aegean,

until they've tramped through the bush without
enough water, or been left with nothing or given
everything, only to be still hungry, then really,
what is the point?

Most days, I can't even meet their eyes—
afraid they'll search my dark pupils for *happy times*,
afraid they'll look for *never ending* and find, instead,
the wordless language that governs the hunt,

afraid they'll see past nice to my inner falconry.
They'd break in all that silence. So I keep it:
how sure I was. How I fell in love with rooftops,
and not for the promise of jumping.

How I longed to be close to the stars
that looked so nice woven atop the Charles,
but that now seem to simply dangle
in their distant hierarchy of burning.

You Still Believe In Me

You Still Believe in Me

Tim Tomlinson

Out this window,
past the pool, the sea, the sun,

I see everything.
I mean,
        God,

and layers of voices
that don't end, or begin.

I put my hands in them.
They express everything
        inside

and I see
what I will do to you

again

and how I won't mean it,
and how I can't help it,
and how that matters to me,

but not you
there

in our bed
where you sleep
at sunrise.

Listening to the Beach Boys Through the Magnetic Fields

George Yatchisin

They share that love
of tinny piano that makes
you want to mispronounce piano
that makes your heart ache
in the way suddenly
aching is glorious.

Tinny isn't far from teen, is it.
Your first heart hurt
is when you discover
your heart, and that
isn't much different
than a genius plucking
at a harpsichord's strings
with a bobby pin,
probably one your love
lost as her hair let loose,
the exact agonizing weight
of first falling in love.

Now a teen thrice over
there's still a part of me
that stirs at the idea
there's such harmony
for hurt—I mean who
doesn't want to wish
its bruised beauty.
Which might be why

I prefer to turn to later
takes on such agony,
ones less studio studied,
ones whose no less
tremulous bridges sing,
"You won't be happy with me,
give me one more chance,
you won't be happy anyway."

You Still Believe in Me

Robert Balun

{See adjacent page.}

I keep seeing myself

walking around

an elusive

oscillating

between

facets

of time

and history

lost in the noise of

just now

reverberating

past the present

visage

a frequency
attuned

as fragile as you

That's Not Me

I had to prove that I could /
Make it alone now, but that's

Jon Tribble

not me. One hand holding tight the other so a blue and silver helmet remained protection, not weapon, not the way to make a bad night worse, hurt not injured and broken, irreparable and bloody, and I knew being in this moment meant I took more wrong turns than just riding my motorcycle after a half pint bottle of Crown Royal and more anger than I could handle then or later or now. Three boys to men, or at least we thought we were in the Walnut Terrace Apartments, first and last month's rent paid, Kevin twenty-one and on the lease, but Paul and I already nineteen going on forever and at least for me more disappointment than the songs we made mix tapes and blasted from Paul's Cutlass Supreme would tell. "Get Up, Stand Up," "You Shook Me All Night Long," Devo and Devo and even more Devo, anything we thought was rebellion, raw bravado for us no matter what the songs really were— Eagles and Eddie Cochran, even those early Beach Boys blasts, Chuck Berry ripoffs stinging our Arkie ears with swagger, surf, bikinis, those album photos of clean-cut boys with rapists' smiles, who could be us. Our jobs as ushers barely paid the rent, but Kevin was assistant manager and could get us all the hours we needed in our black slacks, white shirts, black vests and bow ties; Paul brought all the women with him, a smaller version of Fonzie who had girlfriends enough both Kevin and I found our next from Paul's always friendly second and third runners up. I brought the sound, had spent my college scholarship money on the most amazing Klipsch speakers and a wall of albums both roommates added their relatively meager number. Each would join me and pile titles on when I went for record-store buying binges and there was nothing I didn't want to hear those days, classic and new wave, punk and blues and jazz, hard rock and terrible soft ballads like Bread because I didn't know how but I knew music was the real key to girls and girls were the real key to life as I knew it and felt it, so when she came along, early eighties love of Grease and Gap Band, Journey and Dan Fogelberg, the

Sugarhill Gang to get low to in a Southern girl-who-wasn't-Molly Hatchet-and-mudding, I was lost and didn't understand she was sampling, trying on several sizes, shapes, and styles, and I was one of a half-dozen or so. Her best friend told me come summer I wouldn't be necessary anymore, but I couldn't listen because the fog of sound around me felt as good as when we wrapped into each other and made the night go away. When one of the twins from work who I could never tell apart became her latest thing, I sulked in the apartment, poured shot after shot while her friend watched then left, taking one set of my motorcycle keys with her but not knowing about the spare. How I rode two miles to the theater I don't know, what I did when I was there I'm not sure, how I made it on my bike to start to ride back home, I think—the more time, the more the whiskey took my blood—all I do know is I found myself in the backseat of the car her parents had bought trying not to throw up while both she and the towhead twin kept talk, talk, talking at me, some blather that would make everything better while the only thing real to me at the moment was the helmet in my grip and the back of his head that I could vividly imagine being all the satisfaction I wanted right then if skull and helmet made contact in reverse, outside wrecking inside and my rage, my smile then complete and perfect, damning and wrong. But I didn't, let my face sink between my knees and they took me home, both supported me up the stairs and left me on the couch where my night had started. Alone, I crawled to the stereo, found *Pet Sounds* among those carefully alphabetized albums, and stared at the goats until I felt I was one of them feeding mindlessly on whatever the generous and merciful men offered, pushing away my kind while we all desperately fought for any scrap to fill our emptiness. I managed to put side one on the turntable, skipped past "Wouldn't It Be Nice" and "You Still Believe in Me" since I knew now what lies they were, hopeful stupid lies, and I scratched the tone arm over until I cut the stylus in, found my own true pathetic anthem, waited for Mike Love, yes, fucking Love, to begin to sing my song. "That's Not Me."

That's Not Me

Denise Scannell Guida

Her '69 Nova 8-track only plays the Beach Boys
Adult in the car, she sings the lyrics in a soft voice
only the shotgun passenger hears
Behind her, teenaged girls scream the chorus
"Help Me Rhonda, Help, Help Me, Rhonda"

She releases swells of smoke from a deep inhale
Long ashes overflowing a neglected tray
I breathe a woman's smoke
I see her golden, flipped out bob fanning dry air
as the sun burns her freckled neck

She is no mother I know
She is Caroline, Barbara Ann, the little Surfer Girl
who breaks the beach boy's heart
The stepmother all the girls want
And no one can have

I hear her in lyrics I will soon understand
Her American tongue mocks my old world
of silence about all I wish I knew
Her cigarette conducts a symphony
of school dances, poodle skits, first kisses, and sex

Foot off the gas, she glides on monophonic sounds
Her trembling hand staggers from the wheel
to lift a familiar cup toward her lips
The rearview mirror disguises a paralyzed smile
as she sees my reflection of the girl she used to know

Don't Talk
(Put Your Head on My Shoulder)

Don't Talk (Put Your Head on My Shoulder)

Ken Pobo

Jerry and Jeff argue about
Pet Sounds. Jeff says it's not only
the greatest Beach Boys album,
but the greatest album. Ever. Jerry sniffs,
prefers Wild Honey—Pet Sounds
Is like a dog bred for shows.

The house shivers
as they throw insults and accusations.
The louder they get, the more
they realize that they're fighting
over music they agree on.
They each love both albums.

Winded, they sit on the glider,
watch dusk drip into night.
Fireflies make the buddleia look
like a radio station transmitter
hides in blossoms. Don't talk,

says Jeff. Jerry gets quiet,
puts his head on Jeff's shoulder.
The quiet is like a window
that no one can break.
If only for a few hours.

Evening slips away like a needle
finding the run-out groove,
the last song lost in darkness.

Don't Talk (Put Your Head on My Shoulder)

Susana H. Case

Beaches in New York City aren't like
beaches in California.
There are never as many blondes.

My high-school boyfriend stumbled
through English,
but he knew how to dance—
he could do the Hanky Panky—and he knew
how to reset the odometer
in his father's Ford. Forget classes;
Far Rockaway here we come!

I cram-tutored him for his Regents exam;
all those language lessons
we traded for sand. I'm the daughter of
an English teacher. He got to this country
when he ducked under a fence and ran.

Right before graduation, we walked
for the last time
along the water, looking at shells
washed up by the tides.
"Being here with you feels so right," he sang.
On the way over the Cross Bay Bridge,
Don't Talk (Put Your Head on My Shoulder)
had flowed out of the car radio.
Not good to dance to. But with waves
nuzzling our toes, he remembered
all the lyrics and his grammar was perfect.

I'm Waiting for the Day

I'm Waiting for the Day

Amy Lemmon

The words say I'm the sweet and loving guy
who cares about your broken heart
but the beat says Come here.
The beat says Kiss me.
The beat says I wanna fuck you all night long.

Every girl has her wound,
irresistible to the mortal man

He waits, oh yeah, he waits
till she can love again—
when she does, of course, it's someone else
she loves, not him.

His plaint rises in pitch and volume,
the other voices tangle around,
tethered to the beat. You didn't think—
You didn't think—

There is no thinking here. The flute
and English horn say, Poor girl.
The strings say, Poor poor boy.
The timpani and bongos:
Right now Right now Right now.
Guitar and bass:
If I can't have you no one will.

The woman knows her own
broken heart. It wants
what it wants. What he knows
is waiting, waiting,
waiting still.

Waiting for the Day

Jon Tribble

When anything outside took four years
to make it to Arkansas, even Little Rock,
my sister buying *Pet Sounds* in the spring
of '70 meant we got a taste of the Summer

of Love only three years late, but her nine-
year-old hips were hopping and swaying
mostly to "Sloop John B," "Wouldn't
It Be Nice," a little time on side two

wearing down the grooves to "God Only
Knows." A five-octave boy, nothing
in lower registers, but on "O Holy Night"
I sang like a Wiener Sängerknaben angel,

my mother testing and testing me with
the piano my sister had taken lessons
on to play for years, and no castrati
could soar higher than me, so my shame

was all the greater when I failed to take
the lead in the first-grade production
of "Caps for Sale," couldn't even land
the part of the monkey because they

wanted finger snapping in the audition
and my stubs were useless crab claws
betraying my every effort to syncopate
a copacetic turn and I wept and hated

everything about music for a while.
But when my sister's friend Michelle
took me into my sister's bedroom,
began to undress and dress me, silk

paisley shift replacing my white T-shirt
and jeans, only my Fruit of the Looms
and neutral equipment underneath and
she kept me barefoot like a proper

hippie since we didn't have sandals
small enough for my seven-year-old
feet, piled on the polyester scarves
my sister tied her hair with, on me now

in a pink, orange, blue, red, green, yellow
rainbow. I was a pliant doll, unaware
when she put on the track "I'm Waiting
for the Day," stepped to me as drums

beat out something I didn't know then
was the way a ten-year-old heart
could signal it was broken, and she
took me in her arms, and against

her sobs I wanted nothing but that
pulse, those voices rising as anger
and want found song sinking into
hopeless strings until the drums lifted

me back and I hummed along with
doo doo doo doodoodoo, holding her
until the only sound was crackle
and static leading us to the next music.

Don't Talk
(Put Your Head on My Shoulder)

Let's Go Away for Awhile

Let's Go Away for Awhile

D. Gilson

I want to believe in God and Brian Wilson
and C major to minor fifth, but no, I can't tell you
what that means, fingers spread across the neck
of some guitar not unlike quantum jumps
(the transition of an electron from one quantum
state to another through the absorption or ejection
of other electrons, these mysteries dismissed
by my lacking enthusiasm for physics textbooks
or any deep reading of music theory). This could
be a poem about Brian Wilson and God
giving him chord progressions in the desert
of an acid trip. Pop music has been exhausted,
Brian said, The innocence has been exhausted.
In 1966 my dad was exhausted when his first wife
shipped Pet Sounds to the airbase in Hanoi.
Montreal beat Detroit in the Stanley Cup
finals and The Sound of Music took home
the Oscar for Best Picture. So it was a bad year
unless you were Canadian or Julie Andrews, the worst
year if you were Vietnamese. By all accounts,
it was a good year for the tenor saxophone,
featured prominently in "Let's Go Away
For Awhile." (I'm writing a poem with 264 words,
but in 1966 Brian wrote a song without any
and described it as The most satisfying piece
of music I've ever made). Over coffee at McDonald's
I ask my father about Hanoi and he squeezes
a tiny, plastic cup of creamer between his right
thumb and forefinger until it bursts with a minor plop.

He points to the puddle on the table, then sops it up with his sleeve, Let's go get your mother.

Let's Go Away for Awhile

Tim Tomlinson

but where?
I don't surf, I barely swim,

but I know this sandbox
where there's a grand piano
and good vibrations

and every button on the jukebox
plays "Be My Baby."

Come—we'll laugh
at yesterday.

(I want to cry.)

Let's Go Awhile for Awhile

Corey Oglesby

I think I need to lay down with the person I don't want to
be anymore—run my hand through his hair, tell him

it's been real, but I really need him
to not be real anymore—he'll understand, know

a shit circus like his always leaves town at some point
though he'll probably ask for a last glass of water, linger

in the tiny John Wayne doorway
I built him back in the good ol' days, talking

about the good ol' days—back when we'd hold crooked
menthol cigarettes up above the shower curtain

assembling narratives for betrayals out of boot prints
we'd found in new snow around the building—getting cheap

bleach-burnt revenge in bar bathrooms
wearing only a laurel wreath of victimhood—bawling drunk

afterwards in the blue outer space of an out-of-service ATM
while sleep waited in a plastic baggie across the street

in an unmarked Crown Vic humming Pet Sounds
and a morning bird announced: Yes, you have pissed yourself—

nobody spills a drink in a perfect oval on their lap—
and I expect I'll change, in that moment,

my mind, or lose it in his sad blue eyes, maybe offer him
an over-easy—I'll apologize when I snag-open his yolk,

though I expect he'll say: It's okay,
it was going to break at some point anyway—
       and we'll eat.

Let's Go Away for Awhile

David Starkey

Probably everything will be all right
when we return:
                    the stereo
will being playing *Mantovani's Golden Hits*,

the heart-shaped hot tub in the master bathroom
will once again shoot forth its jets,
                              and the sunburst
clock above the living room mantel will tell
faultless time.

          It's just that now I hear
sounds I don't believe are meant for human ears,

and my mind grows so sluggish

I can only sit here staring
at my reflection in this window
as day vanishes
                    and the rare breaks
from blackness are nothing but airplane lights.

If we're gone,
though,
         the melody can unspin itself,

the horns can find their way back
to the home key,
                    the bells
can ring themselves to the sleep.

So pack a suitcase
and stow it in the trunk of the Porsche.

Bring my pills
and a sheaf of staff paper—
it's useful for starting fires.

If you look in the back of my bottom drawer,
there's plenty of money for exigencies.

Call no one.
            You drive.

God Only Knows

God only knows

Rishi Dastidar

It starts, it always does, as this thrum,
this throb, this itch—this insistence,
this thing of noise and light and love,
that has to force its way out of synapse |
neuron, down nerve << all the way <<,
slithering up and around shoulder, down
arm, through elbow, looping around wrist,
impulse tighter and tighter, swing and swoon,
dip high and dive low until the final
swinglungeburst as the fingers are fired—
tired of hovering over the expectant keyboard,
black and white eyes open, demanding
to be dazzled, Brian. Down they come.
Let them play. Let it play. Let them
have their say—and they say that someone
in London 31 years later will share that
epiphany while standing on an up
escalator at an Underground station,
will think of the person they loved,
will open their arms to their world again,
knowing that everything will be alright
at least until they reach the ticket barrier.

without you

Bonnie Emerick

the heart is a new and selected place
where items accumulate
emotion

my dream had such an air
of sex that I didn't

want it
so I wrote it

this was not
a dream to live in

houses too close
to one another

fences with gates
keeping no one

out

in my future
an energy snare

circulates among people
who pilfer anything I have

without you

"The world could show nothing to me"

M. L. Liebler

The way you look at me,
And smile lets this crazy world roll
On a wave out to sea. Heaven

Is beach where white caps fold our spirits
Together moving towards a silent shore,
Of love tiny fingers through fine sand.

Only God knows the grace of our love
A bright sun star in the night
Bringing fun, surf and hope.

We drive on in blindness waiting
For a convertible of wind to raise
A sail carrying us home to quiet peace.

Only Gods Know

Sean Murphy

Your old man made you and then tried
to end you, the oldest story in the book.
He knew those ancient myths, immortal
through stories lost and gone, all about
Heroes & Villains. Kronos knew the score:
Father is the child of the man, they'll try to
kill you or else become you—so arrest that
development and swallow each one-two-three,
absorb and keep everything inside the family.

Achilles in California, head buried in the sand,
a son willed to success, out of tune but blessed
with an attenuated ear—molded in trials by fire
or more banal brutalities: a 2x4 or fists or worse,
words. Reborn in the salty wake with everything
you couldn't hear and all you could: harmonies
from heaven, the mysteries within Adam's apple—
a towering babble your own brothers didn't divine,
leaving a wrecking crew to launch a thousand songs...

(And wasn't Noah simply obeying orders? Surf's up:
Bad vibrations flooding a sinful earth, his sloop one
big barnyard catching a wave on top of the world?)

Your own symphony to God: wouldn't it be nice?
Bringing down the walls with the sound of a Smile.
Hang on to your ego! Arrogant Icarus, he fucked
with the formula, flying too close to the source, got
burned; or Sisyphus with his Endless Summer, or

Samson, whose prayers buried him in rolling stones?
A half-crazy conductor (for the record), Fate finds you
consigned to a sandbox, bearded and full-bellied,
a god in decline, ill-advised and alone—a castaway.

I Know There's an Answer

I Know There's an Answer

John Davis

More than a breeze at noon
    the bass harmonica
blows across the pasture
    through lazy stems of hay
over the rise and fall of earth.

It blows the fuzz notes
    up and under the fireweed.
Not the great grunts of thunder
    these notes
are the singeing of bees

around a hive
    sweet-scented tones
that buzz and buzz
    blessings of sound
answers we know.

Unlike Brian Wilson

Brendan Stephens

I've never felt
transcendent,

but I understand
the ache of hunger

and aloneness
and want that drove

him to eat acid
to see a schematic

outside his skull—
mapping out existence

like an omniscient
cartographer—if only

everyone shared the trip
that made him cry out,

I know there's an answer
I know now but I have

to find it in myself,
then life in that terrible

gray matter, soft as boiled
tofu, would be more

than a cavern
of bone, a safety zone.

I Know There's an Answer

Tim Tomlinson

but how can I find it
if I don't hang on to my ego,
Mike-fucking-Love?

Here Today

Here Today

Susana H. Case

My smile, well, that encouragement went back
thirty million years, clothes folded carefully,
placed on a desk, earrings and watch,
for ignoring time, on top. You could coax
my hesitation off, a sloughed pelage, didn't have
to whisper a word. I thought your mouth on my neck
might reveal the canines of a zoo babirusa,
or the possibility of slashing sabers of a wild pig,
yet you were so gentle, lips soft like good Irish linen.

You were afraid of leaving bruises; I was afraid
those lips would disappear. And now they have.

Outside, two drivers claim a parking spot,
indecipherable harangue and horns. Somewhere,
a dog barks. It's the tomorrow. You are a camera,
a redacted file. To list your faults, I need a tambourine.
My lips are the color of my crackling synapses;
cherry is how they would light up an EEG.

I'm the Girl He Left Before You Found Him

Kestra Forest

Try not to cut yourself

on his edges:
the serrated geodes that embellish

bites out of his pulpy heart.

On the weekends
he smokes cloves, & when you're not watching,

cherishes them

like a soft hallelujah.
When you look at him, you will see

fertile hurt

bottled behind bright eyes:
so much like families coming one by one

to wash their fresh dead.

He is surrounded
by the Latin names of obscure

Saints: anticipating

a stained glass wink.
You will lose him to booze

& sleep; then find him

in bed, early evening,
late light molten through drapes,

chasing down

unrequited dreams.
As the brass bells of apathy ring & ring,

Trying not to remember
things as they were.

Here, Today

Gerry LaFemina

A brand new love affair is such a beautiful thing...

Her hair the color & texture of grackle feathers
the woman at the table beside mine waves
to a friend on the street. I've fallen in love
with Dublin today, even with the cackle & *caw
caw* of seagulls on St. Stephen's Green,
which could be the name of a shade of green
noticeably different than St. Anne's Green or
Phoenix Park green. I've fallen in love, too,
with the way raindrops freckle the sidewalks
one moment, then sunlight sets the whiskey
in my tumbler luminous. As well with the word
tumbler, which I will not look into the origins of.
I want to raise my glass to that woman,
not because I find her attractive or I'm lonely
in the way of tourists & transients, but because
we're both here, today, a Thursday, afternoon
& our waiter has left us alone. Lovers
parade past, walking close, even that pair of seniors—
how gently he holds her arm to steady her.
Maybe Tony Asher got it wrong. I could watch
musicians play songs their fathers knew,
their grandfathers, or else see the Blackrock
Boys cover the Ventures, Jan & Dean, the Surfaris,
the Beach Boys. They insist the surfing's great
a bus ride away in Dublin Bay, no need
to go to the west coast despite the famous swells
off Donegal & Sligo. Everything old is new again

or so the saying goes, even this city,
even desire, even the green that fills
the sycamores so that I want nothing more
than to be here, by myself, where the faint
keyboard & guitar & tambourine tumble from
a neighboring pub when the door opens,
the Blackrock Boys imploring in harmony
with slight accents we *keep in mind love is here, today
tomorrow it's gone*. Or I'll be gone. There's only
this moment. I can't bear to try a whiskey
called Writer's Tears, but I've tasted the Red Breast,
the Yellow Spot, the Method and Madness. How
satisfying this Green Spot's sweet smoulder when
I take another sip. I've fallen in love with anonymity.
At the other table only her empty wine glass
remains, pink lipstick stain on its rim the only kiss.

I Just Wasn't Made for These Times

I Just Wasn't Made for These Times

Joey Nicoletti

I keep looking for a place to fit
where I can speak my mind
 and the sultry air and perpetual smell of wet garbage
makes me gag. The exhausted owl's hoot
slams shut on the Hummer parked
across the street.

Sometimes I feel very sad.
Sometimes I feel very sad.
The sky slits its wrists
and bleeds refinery oil.

I guess I just wasn't made for these times
or neighborhood streets.

Every time I get the inspiration
to go change things around,
Crazy Craig, my burly neighbor, throws a bag of bones
into my yard. My dog comes running,
then sniffs them, and I take
them away, which makes Crazy Craig
cackle the apples out of his tree.

Sometimes I feel very sad.
Sometimes I feel very sad.
The sky slits its wrists
and bleeds refinery oil.

I guess I just wasn't made for these times
or neighborhood streets.

I Just Wasn't Made for These Times

Glen Armstrong

That suitable place:
The stern faces of strangers

unravel, lightening
as they warm to my insights

on imaginary oceans
and the sounds they make.

I have an orange crate
full of Gatemouth Brown

and Leadbelly. A lot of people
say my head isn't right

because my brain
is a machine that finds its way

without a map. It won't wear
its nametag.

It's a body part that refuses
a mechanical nickname.

Our parents fought in a war
and then sent

us to therapy in their stead.
I was meant

to introduce the electro-theremin
into contemporary gamelan,

to be the great white savior
of the naked Balinese youth,

but now Les Baxter
is knocking at my door

with a film score
and a censor-approved bikini.

Pet Sounds

Pet Sounds

John Davis

The low-key anthem
of night surfing

swirls through a Leslie speaker.
Under a blood orange moon

a surfboard grudges and grinds—
flashes of foam.

Ride inside the black barrel.
Carve the black wall.

What brighter light
than the back beat

of a ride cymbal
a dip and dive a brand

of wit that winces.
This is the path the brain

follows between lost and home,
between conversations

of words baiting their syllables
with violet light.

Pet Sounds

Gerry LaFemina

Rag top weather. End-of-summer light
balanced on the splayed knuckles
of Appalachia. No one here hoards
surf wax or hauls a boogie board
on roof racks of old Fords.
This ain't California. Because
in the market all the talk's of ragweed
or the looming school year or love
—it's finality; its fragility—today
I won't pull over for roadside ice cream.
Let the engine whine: flywheel &
overdrive; rocker arms rocking.
Let wind sweep & acceleration
be my rock 'n' roll. Because I know,
too, the failure of words, believe in it,
actually, I want an instrumental.
The roadster crests another hill;
I steer into an S curve as if barreling
a wave, the maple leaves almost foamy
in the white heat. Even Brian Wilson
understood some moments refuse
harmony, refuse melody, refuse a refrain.
My hair brushed back as if by a woman,
the brow sweat drying, salt
sticky like beach day aftermath.
The road dips & ascends again—
the engine revving, revving
like late night juke box picks,
like your pulse the first time
you fall in love with a song.

Liner Notes

Listening to Pet Sounds

Lisa Kosow

When you listen to Pet Sounds, *use earphones in the dark.*
— Brian Wilson

I disobey, crank up the old speakers
full blast first thing in the morning
drown out dragging morning thoughts
lost in harmonies weaving, wrapped
in sound, I surrender the day to

music from the '60s dreamworld
before Sgt. Pepper's Good Morning
or Sympathy for His Satanic Majesty

Brian Wilson on LSD,
haunted, taunted, by earlier
songs of surfer girls
and surf cities now crumbled
like sandcastles
how close was he to God
only knows how close.

I go on with my day,
tunes get mixed up in my head
I Just Wasn't Made for These Times
I Know There's an Answer

When the Beach Boys Came to Wolf Trap

                              Jacqueline Jules

Two types of tickets were sold—
inside the pavilion and outside on the lawn.
We paid the extra dollars and proceeded
to our sixth row designated seats
under a varnished wood shelter.
The lawn people unpacked picnic baskets
on beach towels under a brutal sun,
too far back to see more than a
miniature of the musicians,
who walked on stage promptly at two p.m.
to open with three upbeat numbers, played
one after another without distracting banter.
I leaned back in my covered seat
and listened to the music beat through
my veins without much thought
to the people in the back, on the lawn,
younger than I, probably not the same
race or religion, certainly not
the same economic class.
An hour passed like that;
then at 3 p.m., I felt a strong breeze
poke my hair and turned around
to see clouds as black
as the drummer's tight T-shirt,
flexing muscles in a growing wind.
Moments later, the sky
dropped a shimmering strobe-light curtain,
drenching the people behind me,
most of whom raised umbrellas

and raced away. Only a few remained
to dance like children under a sprinkler.
 "At least they're cooler now,"
the man beside me murmured,
as we both turned back to watch
the band play just for us,
the privileged in pavilion seats.

Elegy for Brian Wilson's Smile

George Guida

If Brian Wilson won't be happy
                                    how will I?
When a boy of summer cries,
                            how will I
be Loki to Thor?
                    Will sounds be mine?
Will I be sound's?
                    Be happy I was?— or wasn't
his order, or any
                    or sky

or try it this way
                  with more with more
cherubs as castrati,
                  cellos, celestial saws

                  to

let me go home.
                  I feel so, you know,
let me go,
          whatever you are,
my brother singing,
                  Linus reining lions,
stripes on televised shirts
                          flying mini-skirts on stage,
burning ooooooo-
                eeeeeee-ooooooooooo

descending ego,
               ignoring war,
and if God only knew
                          why did only Carl sing?

    And if Mike Love
                          could never love
how can I
               be love, be nice, be loved?
Love can't be.
                    I have no books or poetry.
Just cap and beard
                  protect me, no Apollo
to burn the tempo,
                  to burnish these times.
If you ask, my answer
                  is a girl named Free,
Ra humming so loud
                 you split your skin,
feel it break, so broke up,
                     every time so broke
up, so broken
            the tambourines will say
that's not,
        that can't,
                  just won't be me.

The Other Guy Speaks

Donald Illich

As soon as I heard the timpani,
banging like a hammer on nail,
the harmonies interweaving

over your passionate voice,
I knew it was over. She'd never
return to me, you were victorious.

She'd learn to love again from you.
The flute hovering over guitar,
a helicopter lifting the song's weight,

only guaranteed it. I was the bad guy,
not you, a narcissist who believed
he was the only man for her. Who

told me in no certain terms I was stupid
for thinking she'd ever come back.
But what if she remembered me,

even after all this time, like the violin
in the background, another harmony
to her life that you cannot give her?

True, you had your backing vocals,
your symphony to God, while I was
voiceless, non-existent in your tune.

But that has ended. Forget listening
to your precious music. I don't have
to harmonize to give her what she desires.

I contain everything she needs to thrive —
a look in her eyes, the perfect silence.
Invisible instruments playing our love.

Wilson and Love

Margaret Luongo

Your voice comes through me, I sing what I feel.
My darkness, spite, my lust and jealousy—
I write for you the parts I would conceal.

I play devil, you genius and gentle.
I snarl in the coda, snapping, hungry.
Your voice comes through me, I sing what you feel.

It's hard to love from inside here. I steal
Love when you perform my heart for me.
I write for you the parts I would conceal.

If your rhythm throbs through me, am I real?
I wind myself into your harmonies.
Your voice comes through me. I sing what you feel.

On the road, friend, on the fan's joy you feed,
While I'm trapped, clown horn and barking psyche.
I write for you the parts I would conceal.

It's arranged: on the bridge we meet, equals.
We tug opposite ends of the same lead.
Your voice comes through me; I hear what I feel.
You write the parts for us we would conceal.

How to Work It Out

Andrea Rogers

Don't bother trying. You can't.
The Beatles were wrong;
at least they lied in song.

While we're at it: the Beach Boys
were wrong, too. They weren't even boys,
their surfboards looked unused.

And what's a surf rock anthem,
what are walls of sound, strings swelling
over five-part harmonies

if not an elaborate distraction,
tightly orchestrated expression
of how it feels to be acutely lonely?

I mean, what are pet sounds
if not tiny audible pleas, clearest
articulation of millions of little needs?

When Brian Wilson lost his mind,
he didn't look for love;
he never left the house.

He had a sandbox, a therapist,
hard drugs, music he burned up
in a fit of paranoia. Hell, maybe

he did wish every kiss was neverending
'til the acid wore off and he remembered
he needed his mouth to eat, to breathe.

I know now the difference between a lyric
and a lie, that hardest one to navigate:
Love is All You Need. I don't know

what you need. I never did. How could I know
that pain was a coda of major chords
that would only ever come and come?

How could I know it'd take more than a song
to smooth the scars from falling
off a bike I never learned to ride?

All together now.
Love Love Love.

[still] waiting for the millennium

Vincent A. Cellucci

and how did the city unpack your dreams?
merrily

[dump truck in reverse beeping]

did you divest
    loneliness
        retreat pregnant
         to the one you know best?

[mobile vibrating on the table
pop-up reads papa]

 is there a wrong time to leave?

[stomping the skeuomorph
pedal bell on the light rail]

years don't fall
bang our head on the boulders
we almost let eliminate us
stumbling up the cliff to find a grassy spot
                to crash above
                the break

[sea receding wheeze before rise]

have you ever been
saved with a shove?
[flock of helicopters circles the sky]

if there were only enough shoulders
for all these shushed heads...
I feel sometimes
weren't made for us

[machine welding the warplanes]

I know
the reflection
of the moon
off the savior statue
reaching out to you
don't leave believe in the sand
    deal in desperate
    exfoliate with excrement

[non-existent sound of nuclear fusion]

that's not us

[careful warns the child as we throw
oval eggs in tidal pools
neglecting to peel
prophecies off their shells]

this is how love discloses itself to us
you'll never be without it
answers all

Charlie and The Beach Boys

Ned Balbo

McNeil Island Prison, Washington State, 1966

How did it feel to stand on deck, paroled,
a free man on the ferry to the mainland,
aimless, though in a year you'd find yourself
living with Dennis Wilson of The Beach Boys
and your girls in sunny California,
strumming your songs, the dream within your grasp?
(Two girls hitchhiking on the Sunset Strip—
your girls—would give occasion to connect.)
How did it feel to watch the dream turn sour,
the demo sessions stalled, Brian indifferent
to your off-key voice, the promised contract
still in limbo, Dennis bearded, bored,
your flower-child girls oblivious?
Those dials and switches gleaming on a console
someone else controlled would serve a song
that held your truth: *Submission is a gift*,
cease to exist, plus some love-bead clichés
Dennis would steal because you owed him money
and record, revised, with band and brothers.
By then, you'd moved to Spahn ranch, hangers-on
and homeless kids collecting like the sagebrush
blowing through a movie, always West,
to form a family, somehow, as you led them,
pimp and grifter, prophet of coming war,
through hash and haze... But what else did you brood on,
delusions of grandeur fuelled by LSD?
Maybe that day, still locked up in your cell,

a year before the Summer of Love and Haight-
Ashbury head shops shocked authority,
when, static-chewed, over the wobbly wavebands
of a cheap transistor radio
you heard the far-off voices of a world
unlike your own or any that you'd known—
where strangers—other people—might belong,
all blended vocals, organ, harmonies
grim guards might confiscate at any moment.
You thought, *That should be me out there who's singing,
shaking up the world till it explodes*,
and though you knew release was months away
but couldn't know whose lives you'd one day twist
or ruin or take outright, you hunched in, listening,
humming along with one thought in your head,
hair trimmed, clean-shaven: *Wouldn't it be nice?*

Animal Gospel

Jane Satterfield

The animal gospel abides
in volumes abridged or complete—

the bridal flight of the swarm
spilling across weathered sills,

the crow worrying its rag of mouse,
a needful fable of stab & snatch

—ballad of shrieks & bluster
above the stand of daisies, the heat-

tolerant shrubs. The seasons warm
& tributaries taper off; the cardinal

on the hedge tunes his hearing
toward an anthem of vanishings.

The sheared lawns roll on, pinched off
by picketed gates where surf sounds & sweet

harmonies linger. Upbraid me if I forget
the jade frenzy of grasshoppers

caught in a plastic superstore pouch,
the sleepwalker's sanctuary broken

as the doe threads a stand of oak,
its tonnage pounding the fraught floor.

In me there's an answer, you still believe I know

Cameron McGill

Cut-up/erasure of David Kirby's October 2016 WSJ article, "They Got Around"

NO WORDS CAPTURE the American
frontier society as it progresses
from the history of pop music. This country,
founding the story of California from the inside.
I must be a soldier so my son can be
a poet." Oft-repeated in varying versions—
so his sons and their cousin
can start a band and go from being
(at much greater length) the arc of a special
time in American history..."
Found themselves part of a mastery.
The Boys in catchphrase can be traced:
"I am sending men to the moon.
Our dreamlike, "I must be a soldier
so my son can be a farmer and his son
can be a poet. We lived in that moment"—
era of John F. Kennedy and Lyndon.
Music provided the soundtrack
to the Vietnam War—
warfare to subsistence to the arts—
but suggests how we might view any life really,
connected with the Zeitgeist and withered with the public.
Saints as they were driven, young and American.
"But we weren't treasure seeking, were celebrities
overnight." Our national life, exploited.

"I can't always get a picture. Sometimes
it's pieces. Hard to get less nobodies.
Plain-spoken as presiding genius, wander-
life as son, and supremely gifted.
One of the all-time villains of stage,
his father "generous" and "brutal."
Great promise of endings made public.
They began negotiating part of some
screenwriter's nostalgic longevity
of the Boys. A chart of their career
in which the future president describes
the band: they began with nothing
and in 2012, the Boys celebrated
the revelation that Love follows a hallowed plot,
a childlike ocean spilled on the Beach.

The Beach Boys Come in From the Beach

Lisa Kosow

Hidden in unexpected rooms
violins, harpsichords
pluck out melodies, curtains drawn
songs like sonatas
inside chambers of the heart
quiet damage, andante yet unrestrained,
God only knows what I'd be without you

It creeps up on you, this darkness
after the shattering blast of
we could say goodnight and stay together
that desire, before you're old enough
to know all things fall apart
Caroline No

Deadwax

"Never Much of a Beach Boys Fan"

Gerry LaFemina

I need to say this right from the start: I was never much of a Beach Boys fan. I grew up in New York in the seventies, far from California, surfing, and anyone named Barbara Ann. I was a Beatles fan, then a Stones and Kinks fan, then discovered punk rock, while the Beach Boys were dishing out "Surfin' USA" then "Good Vibrations" then "Here Comes the Night." What I knew of the Beach Boys came from sitting in the back seat of my mother's car when a song would come on the radio "Help Me, Ronda," and "California Girls" or "Be True to Your School," a sentiment I couldn't understand when I was singing along with Alice Cooper's "School's Out for the Summer."

In other words, I didn't get the Beach Boys. I couldn't buy in to their clean cut, cardigan Americana. It wasn't my aesthetic.

In my twenties, I spent time playing in a ska band and in the recording studio, and I became more and more interested in the history of rock and roll. I knew most of the records audiophiles talked about as important: *Sgt Pepper's Lonely Hearts Club Band*, *Exile on Main Street*, *London Calling*, *Highway 61 Revisited*. I knew, too, the non-rock records like *Bitches Brew* and *What's Going On* and *Kind of Blue*. I understood, by then, the importance of production, which is why The Ramones' *Rock and Roll Radio* sounds different (thanks Phil Spector) and what Brian Eno brought to David Bowie on *Heroes*.

Still, by the time *Rolling Stone Magazine*'s 500 Best Albums list came out in 2003, I had never actually listened to *Pet Sounds*. Admitting that brought me incredulous looks from my record-collecting cronies and music loving poet friends. At the time, old vinyl was ubiquitous and inexpensive and I remember finding a fairly inexpensive copy of the record at Mercer Street Books and Records. I looked at it with a bit of disbelief: the goofy cover with the band members feeding the goats screamed 1966, and when I looked at the song list I only recognized "Wouldn't It Be Nice." How can this be so great? I wondered. I don't even know these songs. Still, I spent my $4.99 and took it home.

The fact is, *Pet Sounds* is a terrific record. It's a song writer's record the way certain books of poems (hopefully now this one) are poet's books. That is to say, this is an album that looks at the aesthetic possibilities of the pop song and explores them fully. This record isn't designed to sell records for the Top 40; instead, it is a record of what possibilities the pop song affords. It's both traditional and experimental, and in that way it's very much like my favorite poems. This record is filled with and defines Brian Wilson's voice, his poetics as it were.

For everything that is it is, *Pet Sounds* (which shares initials with Phil Spector, a deliberate allusion to the Wall of Sound) isn't many things. It is not a record filled with radio friendly songs. It is not bubblegum. When I finally played the record I recognized only one other song, and that was "Sloop John B.," the title of which I'd never known. It is a surprise, while simultaneously part of a tradition. It is a Beach Boys record while simultaneously being a Brian Wilson solo record (much of the instrumentation is played by session musicians, leaving only the vocals to the Beach Boys). It is a project, a singular vision as much as *Song of Myself*.

Perhaps that's why so many musicians and poets love this record. The poems in this anthology reflect the diversity of the album and the diversity of the American poetic aesthetic. Keep it new: the Moderns proclaimed. The poems feel new, but listening to *Pet Sounds* yet again, songs I've listened to numerous times by now, I'm astounded that it still feels new a half century later, still feels surprising song to song, now in dialogue with the poems written in their honor. That's saying something.

"More Than Just Surfer Anthems"

Christine Stroud

I grew up on the coast of North Carolina in a small beach town overrun by tourists every summer and completely dead by late September. The Beach Boys were played alongside Jimmy Buffet and John Cougar Mellancamp. Not all their songs, mind you, just "Surfin' USA" and "Surfin' Safari." My friend Heidi had "Barbara Ann" on a tape that had belonged to her mom. We'd dance to them, but even as kids we understood they weren't serious songs. They were fun, silly songs with no substance.

But when I was in high school I read the liner notes for one of my favorite bands citing *Pet Sounds* as an influence. I downloaded it illegally (sorry, sorry, sorry) and listened to the hits, "God Only Knows" and "Sloop John B." I liked it, but I didn't get it yet. I could recognize their catchiness and acknowledge they were more than just surfer anthems, but I couldn't glean any deeper meaning.

It took me another decade to really understand. I was living in a city I hated. I would go out to parties and leave without telling my friends. I would bum cigarettes off people even though I had quit (again). I wanted to be alone in a way I had never experienced. I'd come home late at night and lie on the floor listening to *Pet Sounds* over and over. Sometimes I'd fall asleep down there, waking up to a sore back and a confused cat. These were serious songs dressed up as simple, sweet songs. They were songs that spoke of loneliness and uncertainty in a deeply familiar way. Much like "Letters to a Young Poet," I felt moved to explore the vastness of feeling, no matter how unpleasant it might be. I can trace the wave of my unhappiness in the songs I was drawn to during that period. The early days were all "I Just Wasn't Made For These Times" and "Caroline, No." When the winter ended and I could feel myself moving into a new phase, it was "That's Not Me" and "I Know There Must Be An Answer." By the end of summer, I was sitting on the back porch listening to "Let's Go Away For Awhile" smoking my own cigarettes.

    I thought then, and I think now, about what poets those boys were. Those large and boisterous songs just trying to find the right sound. Those quiet songs seeking to express a difficult sentiment. It's that longing, that playfulness, that fluidity that make this album so rich for a project like this. When I read Katie Mullins's line from the first poem of this anthology,

> But I don't think I realized all those notes,
> those perfect, glowing moments, shot through
> with innocence, would feel so different when
> the rain made our knees hurt and we couldn't eat
> spicy foods before bed anymore…

I thought about the straightforward humanness of these songs that she engages. That sweetly innocent and hopeful song that now means something so different because we're all grown up. Jessica Server's poem about the same tune tell us: "inside the ship's cabin, as I was, vomiting: sometimes vomit is better than nice, too. Bile means alive." Her work plays with the dark moments, it revels in them.

    Amy Lemmon's poem "I'm Waiting For The Day," like Server's piece juxtaposes the innocence and experience. Lemmon gets it. Her poem begins "The words say I'm the sweet and loving guy / who cares about your broken heart / but the beat says Come here. / The beat says Kiss me. / The beat says I wanna fuck you all night long." Like the songs on this album, Lemmon's poem is about duality and desire, about testing limits.

    D. Gilson's poem "Let's Go Away For Awhile" offers the personal blended seamlessly with the political and John Davis's " I Know There's An Answer" captures the song expertly in three short stanzas.

    One of the final pieces in the book, found in the liner notes, "Animal Gospel" by Jane Satterfield, reminds me again the way art inspires. She writes,

...Upbraid me if I forget
the jade frenzy of grasshoppers

caught in a plastic superstore pouch,
the sleepwalker's sanctuary broken

as the doe threads a stand of oak,
its tonnage pounding the fraught floor.

Those lovely lines, those rich images, those reverberating sounds. I'm in awe again and again reading this book because it reminds me again how connected we are and how we all continue to search for more. Like the tracks on *Pet Sounds*, these poems call to us, say "Let's Go Away for Awhile."

About the Poets

Glen Armstrong holds an MFA in English from the University of Massachusetts, Amherst and teaches writing at Oakland University in Rochester, Michigan. He edits a poetry journal called *Cruel Garters* and has three recent chapbooks: *Set List* (Bitchin Kitsch), *In Stone*, and *The Most Awkward Silence of All* (both Cruel Garters Press). His work has appeared in *Poetry Northwest*, *Conduit*, and *Cream City Review*.

Ned Balbo is the author of six books, including *The Cylburn Touch-Me-Nots* (New Criterion Poetry Prize), *3 Nights of the Perseids* (Richard Wilbur Award), *Lives of the Sleepers* (Ernest Sandeen Poetry Prize), and *The Trials of Edgar Poe and Other Poems* (Poets' Prize and Donald Justice Prize). Balbo received an National Endowment for the Arts translation fellowship and was recently a visiting faculty member in Iowa State University's MFA program in creative writing and environment.

Robert Balun is an adjunct at The City College of New York, where he teaches creative writing and composition. His first collection of poems, *Acid Western*, was published by The Operating System in 2020. His poems have appeared in *Reality Beach*, *Powder Keg*, *TAGVVERK*, *Tammy*, *Prelude*, *Barrow Street*, *Apogee*, *Cosmonauts Avenue*, and others.

Susana H. Case is the author of six books of poetry. *Drugstore Blue* (Five Oaks Press) won an IPPY Award in 2019. She is also the author of four chapbooks, two of which won poetry prizes. Her first collection, *The Scottish Cafe*, from Slapering Hol Press, was re-released in a dual-language English-Polish version, *Kawiarnia Szkocka* by Opole University Press. Her work has appeared in *Calyx*, *The Cortland Review*, *Portland Review*, *Potomac Review*, *Rattle*, *RHINO*, and many other journals. She is a Professor and BES Program Coordinator at the New York Institute of Technology in New York City.

Vincent A. Cellucci wrote *Absence Like Sun* (Lavender Ink) and *An Easy Place / To Die* (CityLit Press), and edited *Fuck Poems: an exceptional anthology* (Lavender Ink). He has two collaborative titles: *come back river* (Finishing Line Press) and _*A Ship on the Line* (Unlikely Books).

John Davis s the author of *Gigs* and *The Reservist*. His work has appeared recently in *DMQ Review*, *Iron Horse Literary Review*, *One*, and *Rio Grande Review*. He taught high school for forty years and now performs in rock-and-roll bands, and lives on an island near Seattle.

Rishi Dastidar's poetry has been published by *Financial Times*, *New Scientist*, and the BBC amongst many others. His debut collection, *Ticker-tape*, is published in the UK by Nine Arches Press, and a poem from it was included in *The Forward Book of Poetry 2018*. A member of Malika's Poetry Kitchen, he is also chair of the London writer development organization Spread The Word.

Bonnie Emerick's poetry has been published in print and online journals, including *How2*, *Quarter After Eight*, *Little Red Leaves*, *the tiny*, and *Fogged Clarity*, among others. An electronic chapbook, *Ventriloquy*, is available through The Operating System, and her print chapbook, *Letters Under Vellum*, was published by Finishing Line Press. Her poetry also appears in the anthologies *Selfhood: Varieties of Experience* (Transcendent Zero Press) and *In Corpore Sano* (The Operating System). She teaches secondary English in Telluride, Colorado.

Kestra Forest is a poet in the service job grind with a creative writing BA from Frostburg State University. Her work has appeared in *Backbone Mountain Review* and *Italian Americana* as well as college journals. Sometimes she writes, but she mostly is reading or sleeping.

George Guida is the author of four collections of poems, two volumes of critical essays, and a collection of short stories. He serves as Senior Advisory

Editor to *2 Bridges Review* and teaches writing and literature at New York City College of Technology. A revised edition of his collection *New York and Other Lovers* (Encircle Publications), two new collections of poems, *Zen of Pop* (Long Sky Media) and *All the Photos Never Shot* (Night Ballet Press), and a comic novel, *Posts from Suburbia* (Bordighera Press), will appear in 2020.

Denise Scannell Guida is an associate professor of Communication at New York City College of Technology. Her book chapter, "Environmental Protection Agency Consultations with Indian Tribes: An Intercultural Struggle over the Process of Consent," appears in *Philosophy, Method and Cultural Criticism*. She also co-authored, "Agency through Narrative: Patients Managing Cancer Care in a Challenging Environment," in *Narratives, Health, and Healing: Communication Theory, Research, and Practice*. Her most recent work focuses on Italian American communication. She published two essays, "Amanda Knox and the Bella Figura" and "Memoir of an Italian Nose," in the journal *Italian Americana*. This is her first poetry publication.

D. Gilson is the author of *Incarnate: Notes from an Evangelical Boyhood* (University of Georgia, 2020) and the cultural memoir *Boyfriends* (New York University, 2019). His other books include *Jesus Freak* (Bloomsbury, 2018), with Will Stockton, *I Will Say This Exactly One Time: Essays* (Sibling Rivalry, 2015), *Brit Lit* (Sibling Rivalry, 2013), and Catch & Release (2012), winner of the Robin Becker Prize. An assistant professor of English at Texas Tech University, his work has appeared in *The Indiana Review*, *POETRY*, and *The Rumpus*.

Donald Illich has published poetry in journals such as *Iowa Review*, *Fourteen Hills*, and *Cold Mountain Review*. He won Honorable Mention in the Washington Prize book contest. He recently published a book, *Chance Bodies* (The Word Works, 2018).

Jacqueline Jules is the author of the poetry chapbooks *Field Trip to the Museum* (Finishing Line Press), *Stronger Than Cleopatra* (ELJ Publications), and *Itzhak Perlman's Broken String* (Winner, Helen Kay Chapbook Prize). Her poetry has appeared in over 100 publications including *Innisfree Poetry Journal, Imitation Fruit, Calyx, Connecticut River Review*, and *Pirene's Fountain*. She is also the author of forty books for young readers including the *Zapato Power* series and *Never Say a Mean Word Again*.

Tim Kahl is the author of *Possessing Yourself* (CW Books), *The Century of Travel* (CW Books), and *The String of Islands* (Dink). His work has been published in *Prairie Schooner, Drunken Boat, Mad Hatters' Review, Indiana Review, Metazen, Ninth Letter, Sein und Werden, Notre Dame Review, Parthenon West Review, Caliban*, and many other journals. He is also editor of Bald Trickster Press and *Clade Song*. He is the vice president and events coordinator of The Sacramento Poetry Center.

Lisa Kosow has published poems in *Gargoyle, The Prose Poem Project, Innisfree Poetry Journal, WordWrights!, The Connecticut River Review*, and other journals, and has had poems included in the anthologies *Joys of the Table: An Anthology of Culinary Verse*, published by Richer Resources, and *Cabin Fever: Poets at Joaquin Miller's Cabin, 1984-2001* published by The Word Works. Her chapbook, *Dawn is Moving*, was published by the Argonne Hotel Press in Washington, D.C. She has a BA from Washington College in Chestertown, Maryland, and an MLS from the University of Maryland. She works as a law librarian at the U.S. Attorney's Office in Washington, D.C.

Gerry LaFemina's latest book is the poetry collection *The Story of Ash* (Anhinga, 2018). Both a new chapbook, *Points South* (Hysterical Books, 2019), and a new volume of prose poems, *Baby Steps for Doomsday Prepping* (Madville, 2020), are forthcoming. His previous books include a novel, a collection of short stories, and numerous award-winning collections of poetry, including *The Parakeets of Brooklyn, Notes for the Novice*

Ventriloquist (prose poems), *Vanishing Horizon*, and *Little Heretic*. His essays on poets and prosody, *Palpable Magic*, came out on Stephen F Austin University Press and his textbook, *Composing Poetry: A Guide to Writing Poems and Thinking Lyrically* was released by Kendall Hunt. The former director of the Frostburg Center for Literary Arts, he teaches at Frostburg State University and serves as a Mentor in the MFA Program at Carlow University.

Amy Lemmon was a college radio DJ in the 1980s and her first publication was a poem in *Rolling Stone* in 1986. The author of five poetry collections, most recently *The Miracles* (C&R Press, 2019), her work has also appeared in *The Best American Poetry*, *Prairie Schooner*, *Verse*, *Court Green*, *The Journal*, and many other magazines and anthologies. Amy is Professor and Chairperson of English and Communication Studies at New York's Fashion Institute of Technology, where she teaches poetry, creative writing, and creativity studies classes.

M. L. Liebler was named The 2017-2018 Murray E. Jackson Scholar in the Arts Award at Wayne State University. Liebler is the author of numerous books and chapbooks including the award-winning *Wide Awake in Someone Else's Dream* (Wayne State University Press), which won both The Paterson Poetry Prize for Literary Excellence and The American Indie Book Award for 2009. In 2017, Liebler received two Library of Michigan Notable Book Awards for both his new collection of poems entitled *I Want to Be Once* (Wayne State University Press / Made in Michigan Series) and for *Heaven Was Detroit: An Anthology of Detroit Music Essays from Jazz to Hiphop* (The Wayne State University Press Painted Turtle Series). He was co-editor, with Mike Delp, of *Bob Seger's House: An Anthology of Michigan Short Stories*.

Margaret Luongo is the author of two story collections, *If the Heart Is Lean* and *History of Art*, both from LSU Press. Her work has appeared in *Tin House*, *Cincinnati Review*, *Granta*, the Pushcart Prize anthology, and other publications. Recipient of the Walter E. Dakin Fellowship, the Hawthornden Fellowship, and an Ohio Arts Council grant, she teaches creative writing and contemporary fiction at Miami University in Ohio.

Dawn McDuffie lives and writes in Detroit. She has published poems in *Pearl*, *Feminist Studies*, *Nerve Cowboy*, and *Third Wednesday*. Two of her chapbooks, *Carmina Detroit* and *Flag Day In Detroit*, have been published by Adastra Press. A third chapbook, *Bulky Pickup Day*, was published by Finishing Line Press.

Cameron McGill is a writer, educator, musician, and the poetry editor of *Blood Orange Review*. His poems have appeared or are forthcoming in *The American Poetry Review*, *Beloit Poetry Journal*, *Mid-American Review*, *Sonora Review*, *Willow Springs*, and elsewhere. His chapbook, *Meridians*, is forthcoming from Willow Springs Books. He holds an MFA from the University of Idaho and teaches in the English Department at Washington State University, where he is co-director of the Visiting Writers Series.

Katie Mullins teaches creative writing at the University of Evansville. In addition to being nominated for a Pushcart Prize and editing a rock-and-roll crossover edition of the metrical poetry journal *Measure*, she's been published or has work forthcoming in journals like *Hawaii Pacific Review*, *Harpur Palate*, *Prime Number*, *Big Lucks*, *Pithead Chapel*, *The Evansville Review*, and she was a semifinalist in the Ropewalk Press Fiction Chapbook competition and in the Casey Shay Press poetry chapbook competition. She's also the lead writer and founder of the music blog Katie Darby Recommends.

Sean Murphy has appeared on NPR's "All Things Considered" and been quoted in *USA Today*, *The New York Times*, *The Huffington Post*, and *AdAge*. His work has also appeared in *Salon*, *The Village Voice*, *The New York Post*, *The Good Men Project*, *Memoir Magazine*, and others. He has twice been nominated for the Pushcart Prize, and served as writer-in-residence of the Noepe Center. He's Founding Director of 1455, a literary arts center based in Winchester, Virginia.

Joey Nicoletti's most recent book is *Boombox Serenade*, which was released by BlazeVOX Press. His work has appeared in various journals and anthologies, including *Valparaiso Poetry Review*, *Delirious: A Poetic Celebration of Prince*, and *Drawn to Marvel: Poems from the Comic Books*. A graduate of the Sarah Lawrence College MFA program, he teaches at SUNY Buffalo State.

Corey Oglesby is a poet, songwriter, and visual artist. His poems and poem-comics have appeared recently or are forthcoming in *Beloit Poetry Journal*, *Barrow Street*, *DIAGRAM*, *Hobart*, *Puerto del Sol*, *jubilat*, and elsewhere. Formerly the Editor-in-Chief of *Fugue*, he currently lives in Moscow, Idaho.

Kenneth Pobo had two new books out in 2019: *The Antlantis Hit Parade* (Clare Songbirds Publishing House) and *Dindi Expecting Snow* (Duck Lake Books). His work has appeared in *Hawaii Review*, *Mudfish*, *Nimrod*, *North Dakota Quarterly*, *The Queer South Anthology* (Sibling Rivalry Press), and elsewhere. He teaches English and creative writing at Widener University in Pennsylvania.

Andrea Rogers is a musician and PhD poetry student at Georgia State University, where she is an Advanced Teaching Fellow. She is the recipient of the 2015 Agnes Scott Writers' Festival Poetry Prize, judged by Tracy K. Smith, and two Academy of American Poets awards. Her poems appear or are forthcoming in *The Adirondack Review*, *Exit 271: Your Georgia Writers Resource*, Negative Capability Press's *Stone, River, Sky: An Anthology of Georgia Poems,* Red Paint Hill's *Mother is a Verb* anthology, *Treehouse*, and *Odradek*; her nonfiction and interviews appear in *Boog City*, *Treehouse*, and *The 11th Hour*. She and her band, Night Driving in Small Towns, have been featured by *Rolling Stone* and NPR.

Brent Royster's poems have been published in *Center: A Journal of the Literary Arts*, *Cimarron Review*, *Green Mountains Review*, *Iron Horse Literary Review*, *Mochila Review*, *The North American Review*, *Quarterly West*, *South Carolina Review*, and other notable journals. He teaches at Central Texas College.

Jane Satterfield has received awards in poetry from the NEA, *Bellingham Review*, Ledbury Poetry Festival, Mslexia, and more. Her books of poetry are *Her Familiars*, *Assignation at Vanishing Point*, *Shepherdess with an Automatic*, and *Apocalypse Mix*, winner of the 2016 Autumn House Poetry Prize, selected by David St. John. New poems may found at *The Common*, *Nelle*, *Hopkins Review*, *Interim*, and more. Her poem, "Animal Gospel," first appeared in *Interim*.

Jessica Server is a poet, nonfiction writer, journalist, editor, and educator. Her poetry chapbook, *Sever the Braid*, was published in 2013 and her work has been featured in *Best American Poetry* (Blog), *Proximity Magazine*, *Blue Earth Review*, *Pretty Owl Poetry*, *The Good Men Project*, and elsewhere. She holds an MFA from Chatham University and currently lives in the Chicago area with her husband and son.

David Starkey served as Santa Barbara's 2009-2011 Poet Laureate and is Director of the Creative Writing Program at Santa Barbara City College. His poetry has appeared in many journals and in seven full-length collections, most recently *Like a Soprano* (Serving House, 2014), an episode-by-episode revisioning of The Sopranos television series. His textbook, *Four Genres in Brief* (Bedford/St. Martin's, 2017), is in its third edition.

Brendan Stephens is currently attending the creative writing and literature PhD program at the University of Houston and is the recipient of an Inprint Donald Barthelme prize. His previous work has appeared or is forthcoming in *Epoch*, *Southeast Review*, *Notre Dame Review*, *Carolina Quarterly*,

Smokelong Quarterly, *Into the Void* magazine, *Clash by Night*, and elsewhere. He is an online fiction editor for *Gulf Coast Literary Magazine*.

Christine Stroud is editor-in-chief of Autumn House Press. She has an MFA in Creative Writing from Chatham University, where she earned the Best Thesis in Poetry award. Her chapbook, *The Buried Return*, was released by Finishing Line Press in March of 2014, and her second chapbook, *Sister Suite*, was released from Disorder Press in 2017. Stroud's poems have appeared in Ninth Letter's first web edition, *The Paterson Literary Review*, *Cimarron Review*, *The Laurel Review*, and many others.

Tim Tomlinson's story collection, *This Is Not Happening to You*, has been likened to "licking something bitter from a very sharp knife." He is the author of the chapbook *Yolanda: An Oral History in Verse*, the poetry collection *Requiem for the Tree Fort I Set on Fire*, and co-author of *The Portable MFA in Creative Writing*. He is a co-founder of New York Writers Workshop, and Professor of Writing at NYU's Global Liberal Studies.

Jon Tribble is author of three collections of poems: *Natural State* (Glass Lyre Press, 2016), *And There Is Many a Good Thing* (Salmon Poetry, 2017), and *God of the Kitchen* (Glass Lyre Press, 2016). His next book, *The Automatic Earth*, is forthcoming from Salmon Poetry in 2020. He is managing editor of *Crab Orchard Review* and series editor of the Crab Orchard Series in Poetry published by SIU Press. (Jon passed away in October 2019; this book is dedicated to him.)

George Yatchisin is the author of *The First Night We Thought the World Would End* (Brandenburg Press) and the chapbook *Feast Days* (Flutter Press). He is co-editor of *Rare Feathers: Poems on Birds & Art* (Gunpowder Press) and his poems appear in the anthologies *Reel Verse*, *Clash by Night*, and *Buzz*.

About the Lo-fi Poetry Series

The Lo-fi Poetry Series editors are seeking proposals from potential editors for subsequent anthologies in the series. Each book should cover one record (our focus is primarily on rock-pop-alternative from the 1960s to today)—no best of collections! Anthologies should include "cover poems" of each song on the record as well as "liner notes" poems that engage the record as a whole. Poems may include history, personal reflection, notes about the band's recording of the song or playing it, song fragments, and other ways of engaging the album.

Each anthology proposal should include names and bios of each editor (we seek a minimum of two editors for each anthology), a sample of potential contributors/poems, and a rationale for covering that record. Books based on accepted anthology proposals will be published by CityLit Press, the imprint of nonprofit CityLit Project (http://www.citylitproject.org).

Editors' responsibilities:

- Deliver approximately 80-125 ms pages (including front matter, contributor bios and notes, etc.) on time as determined by publisher upon acceptance of the proposal;
- Obtain written permission from each contributor for one-time use of poem in anthology and related promotion;
- Procure any and all rights and permissions for any reprints as required;
- Suggest, advise on, and/or obtain artwork—and related rights—for cover under publisher's direction (intended to engage or be derivative of original album art);
- Develop release events to promote the book in various literary and music venues;

- Provide series editors with a up-to-date mailing list of contributors; and
- Help promote their book and the series in general.

Publisher responsibilities:

- Make decisions on proposals in a timely manner, and provide a manageable deadline for the anthology editors;
- Print and promote an attractive edition of the book;
- Guarantee two (2) contributor copies for each contributing poet and editors, and distribute those upon release of the book;
- Distribute the book through a variety of means, including wholesalers, select retailers, and on-line venues such as Amazon.com and bn.com.

Send anthology proposals to Lo-fi Poetry Series Editors, c/o CityLit Press attn: Gregg Wilhelm, publisher, at greggutmfa@gmail.com.

Launched in 2010, CityLit Press's mission is to provide a venue for writers who might otherwise be overlooked by larger publishers due to the literary nature or regional focus of their projects. It is the imprint of nonprofit CityLit Project, Baltimore's literary arts center, founded in 2004.

Also Available
Clash by Night
LaFemina and Wilhelm, Eds.
ISBN: 978-1936328-17-8

 Poets Cover Your Record Collection

www.ingramcontent.com/pod-product-compliance
Lightning Source LLC
Chambersburg PA
CBHW081357040426
42451CB00018B/3487